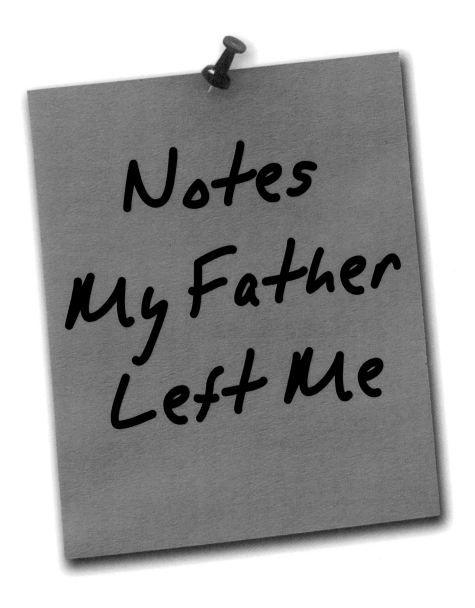

Ray Iallonardo

Archway Publishing books may be ordered through booksellers or by contacting:

Archway Publishing
1663 Liberty Drive
Bloomington, IN 47403
www.archwaypublishing.com
1 (888) 242-5904

Because of the dynamic nature of the Internet, any web addresses or links contained in this book may have changed since publication and may no longer be valid. The views expressed in this work are solely those of the author and do not necessarily reflect the views of the publisher, and the publisher hereby disclaims any responsibility for them.

Any people depicted in stock imagery provided by Thinkstock are models, and such images are being used for illustrative purposes only. Certain stock imagery © Thinkstock.

ISBN: 978-1-4808-2738-7 (sc)
ISBN: 978-1-4808-2739-4 (hc)
ISBN: 978-1-4808-2740-0 (e)

Print information available on the last page.

Archway Publishing rev. date: 3/9/2016

On the cover, Dad, May 2011.

We were just on a layover in New York City from a trip back from Hawaii, so of course I bought leis for everyone as gifts. I had also bought my first iPad in Honolulu, and was explaining to dad that the iPad is also a camera when I shot this photo of him. Naturally, he had no concept that such a contraption could also take photos. I managed to take this photo just as he was uttering "what are ya tawkin' about??"

Contents

Acknowledgements

This book wouldn't have been possible without my family and friends who've read early drafts and encouraged me to keep going. Especially Christopher Capraro, who inspired me to write this in the first place, and then introduced me to editor Matt Kachur, who kept both the book and me in focus.

I'm also grateful for having friends who are there to help me when I call them in panic, like Michael Gorski, who helped me at the spur of the moment with some photos, and Tom Bouman and Inge Schaap, who created the book's website for me.

Thanks also to my friend Patrick Potts who helped me clean out the house and discovered many of these items with me. Also thanks to my sister Donna Sansoucie and my partner Marcel Jansen who lived through many of these experiences and put up with me through all of it.

Finally, thanks to my dad for all this material. Dad, you never thought I had any sense of humor, but I think I did pretty well despite that.

Foreword

After my father passed away in August of 2013, we needed to clean out his home and prepare it for sale.

Over the years, my dad wasn't thrilled to have visitors in the house, so I'd have to explain to friends the antics that went on, especially after my uncle moved in. Then, while cleaning up the house after his passing, you wouldn't believe the things I found. To keep my sanity, I started posting photos on Facebook, because I wanted to share some things that I didn't think anyone else would believe. Then, the posts and photos turned into a nice memory of a home the way my dad kept it, and of a man who lived his life the way he wanted to live it. This book is a result of those postings—memories of my dad.

To quote my friend Christopher Capraro, who read the first drafts of this book:

"Some things today are better today, but let us not forget it
took yesterday to get here."

Chapter 1: Notes

This is the photo that started it all. I was sitting at the dining room table and had to jot down something, and grabbed the closest Post-it®. I noticed that someone wrote "over" on the backside. Evidently, dad felt he needed to make sure which side of a Post-it people should write on!

Here's a variation of the above:

Just in case visitors didn't know how to flush a toilet, this note was placed prominently above it so they'd know how to flush the "correct" way...

And, if you forgot how to flush the toilet in the second bathroom, in case it is different than the first, which it isn't, there's a note for that bathroom too...

After 50 years, you would think locking the same lock wouldn't require instructions......

Don't know what to do with this scary looking, Frankenstein-like switch before going to bed at night?
There's a note...

This looks pretty funny, but it was quite ingenious. Before my dad ate every meal out —either at the
Allerton Diner or at Fratelli's—he used to cook for himself. At times, he would produce quite some smoke
during cooking, thereby setting off the smoke detector. The above switch was rigged to the battery of
the smoke detector. For most of us, we have to climb a ladder or stand on a chair to disconnect a smoke
detector. But my dad would flip this switch off during cooking, and flip it back on afterward. Of course,
this note was long forgotten, because the switch was in the "off" position for quite some time.

At dad's, if you wanted to shred worthless junk mail, there was a place for it. Any piece of mail with any iota of identification – name, address, initials, whatever – needed to be shredded. Of course, that would only work if you actually shredded the material. I found junk mail in this bucket that was over five years old. I guess if you never throw out your junk mail, that's one way of people not stealing your identity.

Just in case you run out of toilet paper. Or, in case the lights go out and you are reaching around for the roll, there is always one on hand at dad's. I've only seen multiple toilet paper rolls in hotel bathrooms, and the most I've seen were two rolls. I think this may have originated because my dad and his brother used different brands. But over the years, I think they adapted to one brand – as most "married" couples do over the years.

These notes from my father to my uncle were pretty funny, and I think also touching that my uncle left the notes up in the year that he lived in the house after my dad passed.

After my dad became less and less mobile, he'd want my uncle to make sure he'd have his cell phone with him, just in case my dad would need to call him when he was out.

The best, though, is "Don't forget the F'n garbage before we go out!" Yes, that is "F'in" as in the f-word. Not sure why my dad needed to describe the garbage that way. But if you knew him, you can hear him saying it.

Just in case you forget you've lived in The Bronx for the last 50 years and need to lock the doors every night...

If you didn't know that the sheet with the elastic around it goes on the bottom of the bed, it was labeled as well. I mean, where else would a fitted sheet go?

In case you didn't know that this box of facial tissues indeed contained facial tissues, it too was labeled. Maybe someone might have mistaken it for toilet paper?

I nearly lost it when I found this note. To put this in context: my childhood room was converted into my dad's office after I moved out in the 80s. I think dad saved every piece of paper, tax return, bill, whatever, since then. This note was found after two or three hours of throwing things out—er, I mean, of "shredding" all of his old paperwork. It still took another half a day of throwing things out after finding this note.

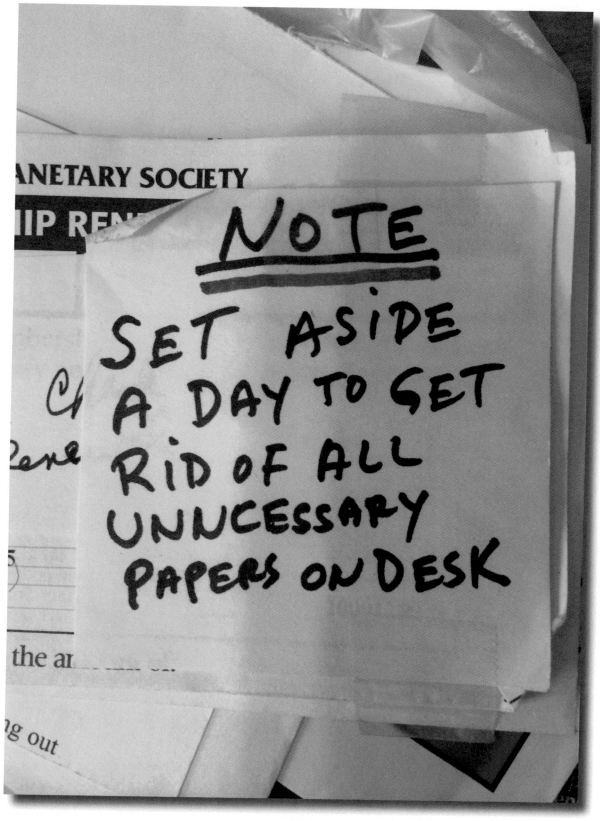

Even I couldn't believe this one!! I never found out what this box was used for—and I don't think I even *want* to know.

I had to get a court order to open dad's safety deposit box. Once I went through it, I found no hidden treasures, only historical documents about the family, which of course are priceless. This, however, was on the same level as the previous photo. Not sure of the logic of storing this at the bank! Yes, it is an empty envelope with the word "EMPTY" written on it—on both sides, no less!

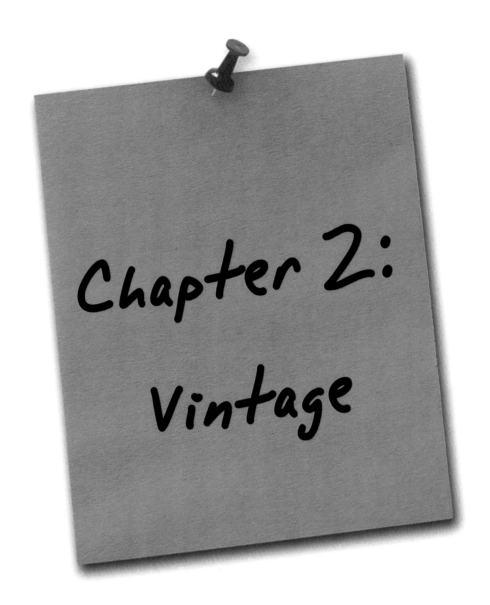

Chapter 2:

Vintage

The items that I found in the house would make a collector drool. Unfortunately, I had no time to hock them on eBay so the fine people at Goodwill will have to try to find new homes for some of these items, such as this combination 8-track player, turntable, cassette deck, and AM/FM radio.

Dad labeled this rotary telephone with one of those little label-makers from the 70s (he loved labeling things). It was for his "Florida" room, which he created by screening in the areas under the porch in the back yard.

This is dad's camp toaster, which he used instead of the regular toaster. It worked quite well, but only when you didn't forget about the bread that was being toasted over an open flame. Since he forgot about it quite often, we're lucky he didn't burn down the house!

My mom's "portable" sewing machine, which weighted a ton!

You remember the old Polaroid Insta-matic, don't you?

This portable typewriter is a classic.

The IBM Selectric, with the letters on the little ball that went back and forth, was a major breakthrough. Dad never understood how a computer or a laptop could beat this.

Perhaps you were thinking dad needed only one portable typewriter?

I hated to see this reel-to-reel tape recorder go!

I'm not sure how this oil lantern came into dad's possession. I don't think I ever saw him use it. Once, he wanted to take it on Cub Scout camping trip that I was attending but because it was an open flame, it was forbidden because the Cubs weren't old enough. I think he must have forgotten about it since then.

23

Christmas 2005

Every Christmas, one of New York City's local television stations, WPIX 11, would broadcast the "Yule Log," which was simply a continuous feed of a lit fireplace, accompanied by Christmas Carols for 24 hours between Christmas Eve and Christmas Day. At some point over the years, my dad started dressing up the TV with brick construction paper and stockings, so that when the Yule Log was broadcast, he'd be all set for holiday cheer. He got the bright idea of taping the Yule Log broadcast (which he then copied and sent to me), so that he could enjoy the fireplace TV anytime during the year. In 2005, he decided to leave the TV dressed as a fireplace all year round.

Christmas 2012

Every Christmas, he must have taken a photo of the fireplace TV because I found so many photos of it. At some point, the photos must have blurred together, so dad decided to label his Christmas fireplace TV by year.

Christmas 2003

My dad thought this photo of the two of us warming ourselves by the fireplace TV was hysterical.

May 2014

Just before being placed outside for garbage collection.

Chapter 3:

Hobbies

Dad's number one hobby was gambling, consisting of playing the lottery, specifically scratch lottery tickets. After scratch lottery tickets, my dad was fascinated with trains, so much so that one of the gifts that he actually kept was this Lionel train wall clock. This clock would signal the hour with the "chugga-chugga chugga-chugga whoo-whoo!" of a locomotive, with the train traveling around the face of the clock.

My father's next hobby was amateur electrical work, evidenced by this device, which turned off the sound of his train clock.

In the 90s, dad "installed" a ceiling heat lamp above the entrance to the shower stall in the bathroom. Fortunately, all wires were above water level. I joke about it now, but I wish I had absorbed some of his electrical "prowess"—I can barely change a light bulb!

This electrical contraption was in his office. Whatever was plugged in, usually a reading lamp or a fan, would be controlled by the doorbell switch, which became an on/off switch.

Here's another variation of his on/off extension cords:

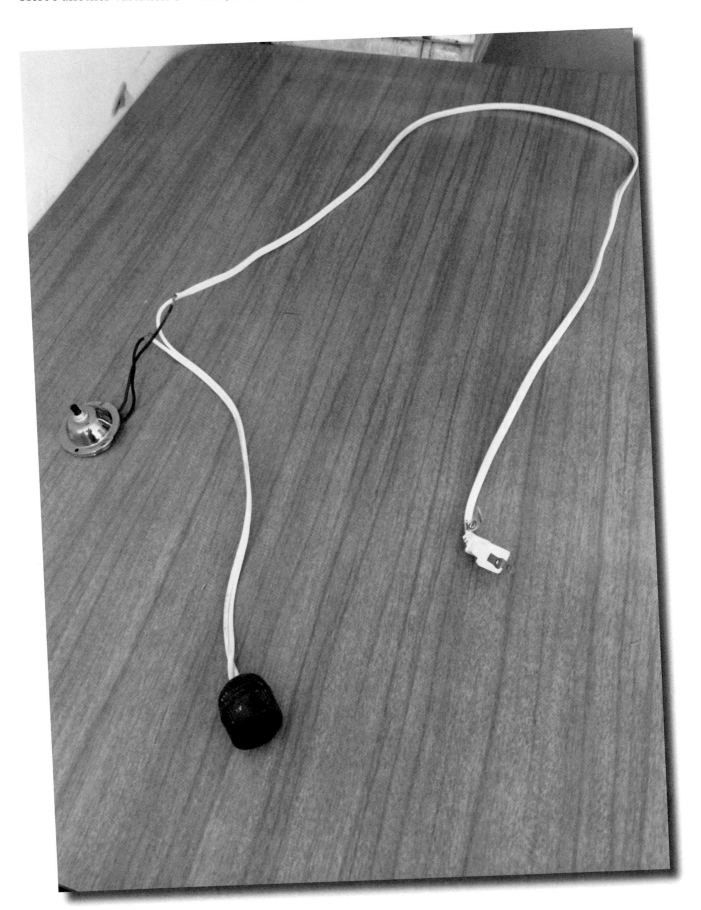

Here's another example (the bottom is a close-up of the top photo—remember those labels!). Dad sure loved those Rube Goldberg-like switches! These controlled the speakers to the stereo in the living room, in case he wanted to turn off just one of the speakers. Not sure why one would do that, but I guess it is good to have the option? I don't remember if the doorbell controlled the speakers or something else—we'll never know. The flashlight was hung so dad could have it nearby in case he couldn't see what he was doing in that corner of the room.

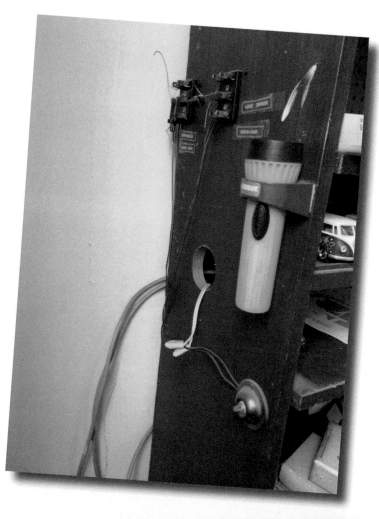

Chapter 4:

Humorist

My dad thought he was the funniest person in the world, but as his son, we hardly laughed at the same things. He was also a staunch patriot. He had this copy of the Declaration of Independence framed and mounted in the entry hall of the house. However…

...in the '70's, he thought it would be funny if we all signed it: me, my sister, my mom, and, of course, dad. Of course, visitors never noticed the extra signers until he pointed them out.

My father had loads of photo albums, usually of his trips to New Hampshire visiting my sister and her family for the holidays or birthdays. In 1999, my sister divorced, and in the middle of his 1999 album, we found this while going through it. We all had a good laugh.

Chapter 5:

Keepsakes

I was surprised at what he kept as keepsakes. Some of them were the few gifts that he actually kept. I already pointed out the Lionel train wall clock, which was a gift from my sister. That was kept because it was train-related, and not necessarily because it was from my sister. Other gifts kept: scratch lottery tickets. That's about it. My sister once bought him an electronic frame and loaded photos of the grandkids, so all he'd have to do was to plug it in. Too complicated. I got him travel-size binoculars for his travels (he traveled as a member of AARP). Too small. When I was in my early 20's, I spent a week's salary on a wrist watch with Roman numerals that he was always talking about, but he failed to mention he wanted it to have a second hand, and of course the one I bought didn't have a second hand. That gift became mine because the small jeweler across from Bloomingdale's wouldn't accept returns.

Clothing was OK, provided it fit his already limited wardrobe, which consisted of white T-shirts, polyester pants (although Dockers were OK), and baggie gray pullover sweatshirts. T-shirts with photos of the grandkids, as well as any mention of gambling or casinos, also were OK. My sister and I knew what to give him after a while, because he refused the unwanted gifts immediately. My cousins who gave him gifts had no clue. These gifts were accepted with a smile and a thank you, but were placed unopened in the closet. You wouldn't believe the amount of unused clothing I gave away to Goodwill. I hope some needy family is happy— provided they all have 42-inch waists and 30-inch pant lengths (the label for which he stuck to his bedroom closet door so he wouldn't forget).

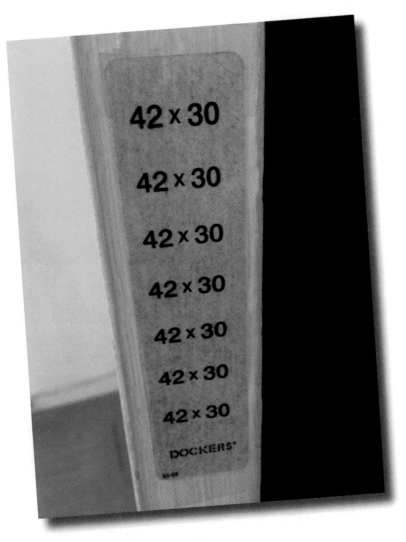

One gift that I thought he'd like, before I knew better, was this wall clock with 3 different time zones.

Whenever he called me in Amsterdam, he'd always ask me what time it is, so I thought it be fun if he had a clock with the different zones. I couldn't find a clock with just New York and Amsterdam, so I found the above, which included Tokyo.

However, my dad had no use for Tokyo, so he changed it. He had much greater satisfaction in knowing what time it was in his Mecca, Las Vegas, than a place as mundane as Tokyo. And simply replacing Tokyo with Las Vegas was not enough—he then had to rearrange the cities in the correct geographical order.

This 1987 wall calendar/tea towel was still hanging in the kitchen in 2014. In 1985, my parents went cross-country, via Amtrak, of course, to California. Well, one-way via train. They flew back, because by then my mom had had enough of the train. I suspect they bought this together, and my dad never had the heart to take it down—partly because of my mom but I'm sure also because of the cable cars, which he also loved as much as trains.

39

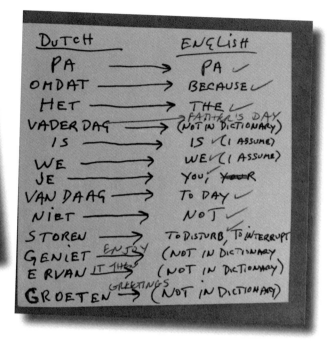

My dad was adamant that I speak Dutch when I moved to Holland—the Italians who immigrated to New York in the early 1900s had to learn English after all—and he wanted me to send him birthday cards in Dutch. He then bought a Dutch/English dictionary and tried to translate them. I found these notes among his papers: his attempts at translations and his note to me indicating that he couldn't translate completely.

I bought this fake scrimshaw letter opener for my dad in the early 70s when my Cub Scout pack took a day trip to Mystic Seaport, Connecticut. I can't believe he saved it after all these years, but I'm guessing he did because it got the job done, and not only for sentimental reasons.

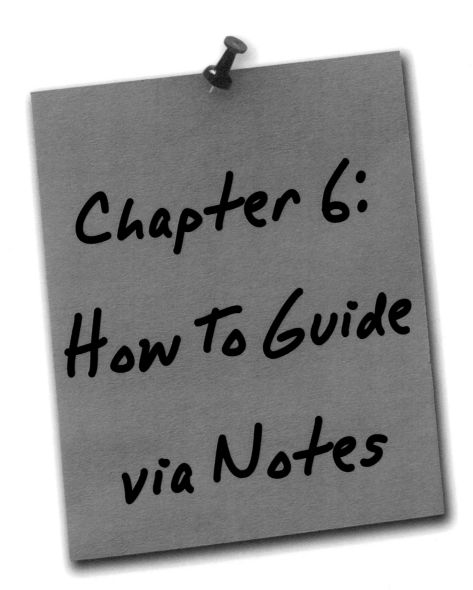

Chapter 6:

How To Guide

via Notes

How to keep a tidy kitchen…if you don't look at the notes posted all over the place…

How to make a beef stew (I've been told that this recipe is pretty good!)...

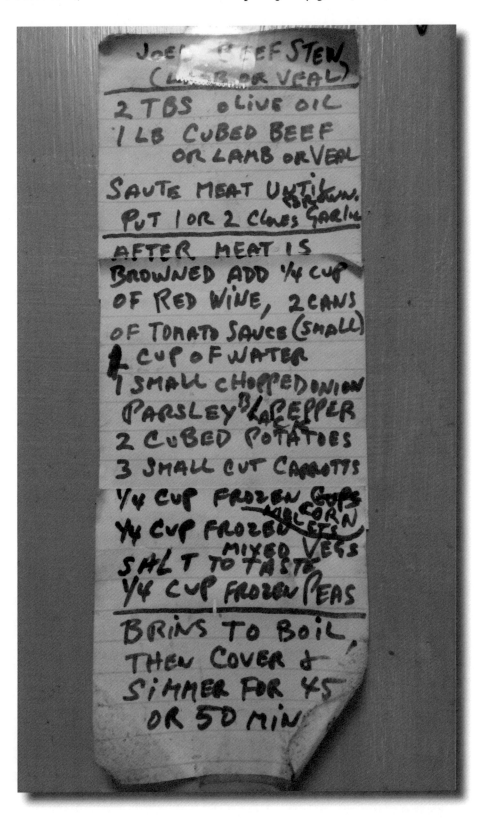

How to use your phone and answering machine.

What to say when you record your outgoing message. I think he re-recorded the exact same message about every six months...

What to say if a telemarketer calls...

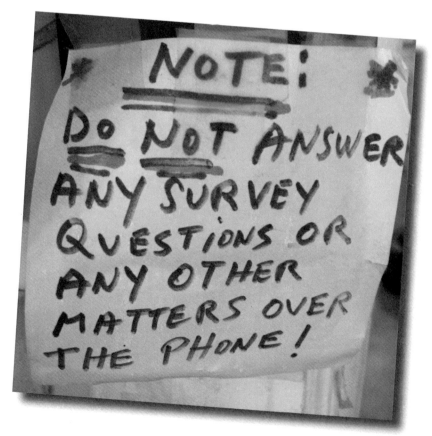

How to change the battery of your cordless phone... (Not sure why "phone" needed to be shortened to "fone." Maybe he was running out of Post-its?)

How to balance your checkbook…

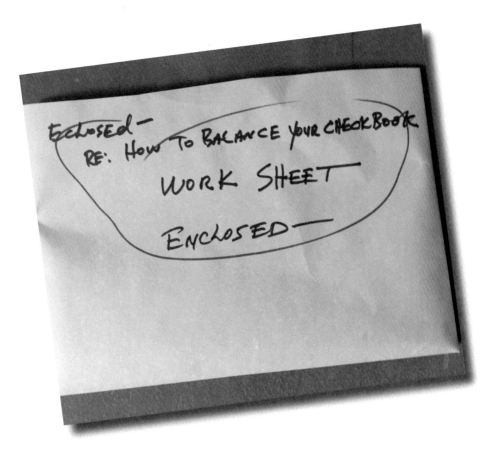

How to remember when you first started using the microwave...

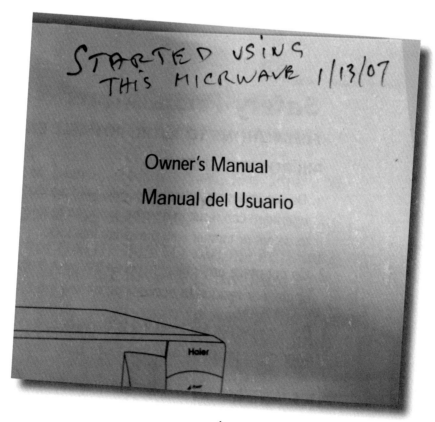

How to remember that this folding chair is yours...

How to remember that there are clothespins in this plastic bin...

How to remember what to say when you go to the dentist...

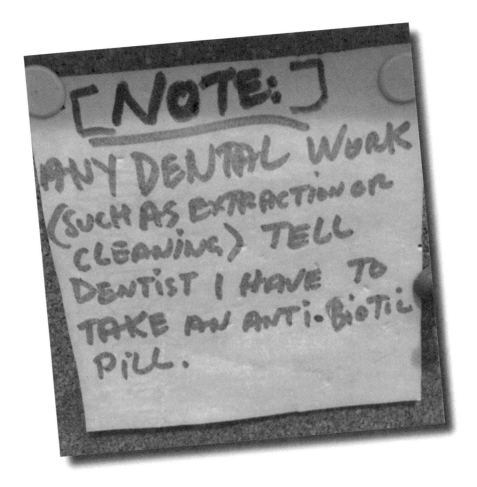

How to set the thermostat in case you've forgotten...

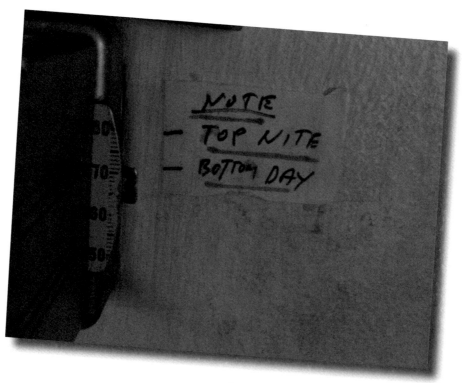

How to pack up a portable burner...

How to remember when to replace the batteries of the smoke detector that used to hang from these two screws, but was taken down years ago...

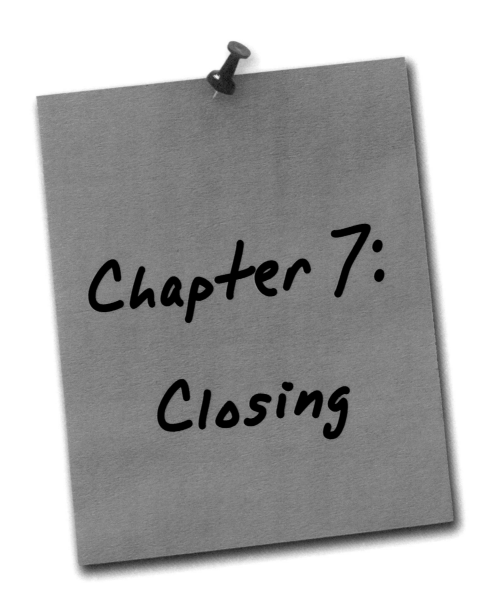

Chapter 7:
Closing

Before he started using Post-its, my dad used this to pin notes to the front door.

After all the "shredding" was done, I felt the "to be shredded" sign needed an appropriate send off, via recycling.

The one thing that would drive me crazy would be the constant blaring of 1010 WINS from the radio, in addition to the TV blasting away at the same time, and the "chugga-chugga chugga-chugga whoo-whoo!" of the train wall clock once an hour. So once the house was empty, I decided to give the radio its final resting place. Not to worry, this radio was not an antique, but a replica made in the late 90's.

The Final Note

Based on the replacement date, I am estimating that this must be my dad's final note. He passed away August 24, 2013.

Dad, 2012, as happy as he can be, with his Foxwood Casino hat and Atlantic City sweatshirt.

Epilogue

Because of his service in the army, my dad was buried with military honors, which included a bugler playing Taps. As soon as the bugler started—almost on cue—a nearby Metro North train passed and blew its horn through the entire piece. As my dad loved trains as much as he loved his country, we thought this was very appropriate.

I became especially emotional during the service when the honor guard handed me the folded American flag and thanked me for dad's service by saying "On behalf of the President of the United States..." Even though my dad would have rolled his eyes at the mention of a non-Republican president, I'm sure he would have loved the ceremony regardless.

How fitting it was that the buyers of the family home were a veteran and his family. I think my dad would have liked this, and I hope the new family will be able to build new memories and cherish them as much as we have, with or without notes.

About the Author

Ray Iallonardo is originally from The Bronx, NY, and has lived in Amsterdam, The Netherlands since 1998. He is proud to have lived most of his life in two places that are both identified with a definite article. *Notes My Father Left Me* is his first publication.

Printed in the United States
By Bookmasters